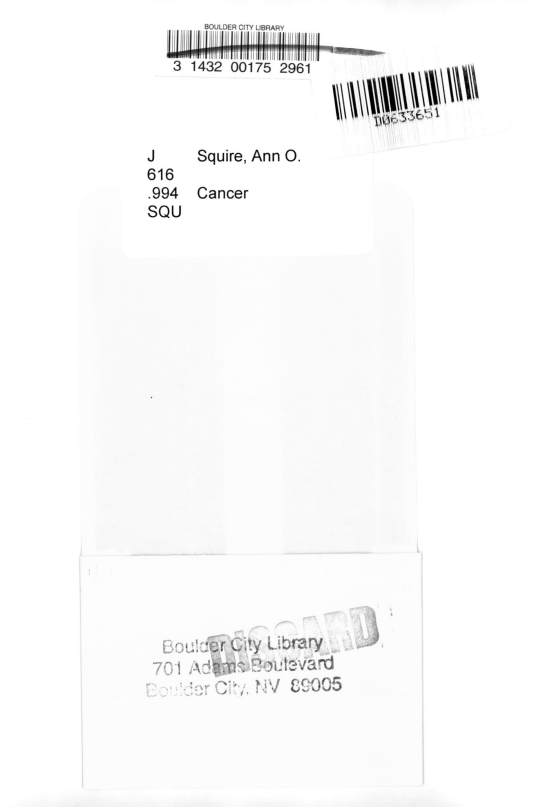

Cancer

ANN O. SQUIRE

Children's Press®
An Imprint of Scholastic Inc.

Content Consultant
Karen E. Peters, DrPH
Clinical Assistant Professor
Division of Community Health Sciences
University of Illinois–Chicago, School of Public Health
Chicago, Illinois

Library of Congress Cataloging-in-Publication Data
Squire, Ann O.
  Cancer / by Ann O. Squire.
      pages cm. — (A true book)
  Includes bibliographical references and index.
  ISBN 978-0-531-21472-5 (library binding) — ISBN 978-0-531-21522-7 (pbk.)
1. Cancer—Juvenile literature. I. Title.
  RC264.S68 2016
  616.99'4—dc23   2015003913

Front cover: A large group of people form the shape of a cancer awareness ribbon

Back cover: Cancer cells

Find the Truth!

Everything you are about to read is true *except* for one of the sentences on this page.

Which one is **TRUE**?

T or F Cancer is not contagious.

T or F Cancer is always fatal.

Find the answers in this book.

Contents

THE BIG TRUTH!

**Cigarette smoking is the
leading cause of lung cancer.**

Sunblock helps prevent skin cancer.

X-rays and other images
are often used to determine
if a person has cancer.

5

After school, Carrie was thrilled to see that Aunt Sue was visiting.

CHAPTER 1

What Can It Be?

It was almost 4:00 p.m. when Carrie left school and began the short walk home. She had stayed after class to work on a science project, and she was afraid her mom would be upset that she was so late. As she approached the house, she saw her Aunt Sue's car in the driveway. Carrie's mom and Aunt Sue were sisters, and they spent a lot of time together, talking and laughing. Carrie ran to the front door, excited to see her aunt.

There are more than 14 million people in the United States living with cancer today.

Aunt Sue's News

When she entered the kitchen, Carrie could tell that something was wrong. Her aunt's eyes were red and puffy, as if she had been crying. Carrie's mom was leaning forward and talking softly. Both looked up as Carrie came in. "Is everything OK?" she asked. Her mom nodded. "Why don't you go and start your homework, and I'll be up in a little bit." As she climbed the stairs to her bedroom, Carrie wondered what could be going on.

Though she had plenty of homework to do, Carrie couldn't concentrate knowing that something was going on with Aunt Sue.

When people have medical troubles, sometimes they need comfort from a friend or relative.

After a time, there was a soft knock on Carrie's door. Her mom came in, looking sad and serious. She told Carrie that Aunt Sue had been taking a shower that morning when she noticed a small, hard lump in her breast. She was afraid that it might be cancer. Carrie's mom had suggested that Aunt Sue make an appointment with the doctor.

Carrie was really worried. She had heard about cancer—it was a very serious disease.

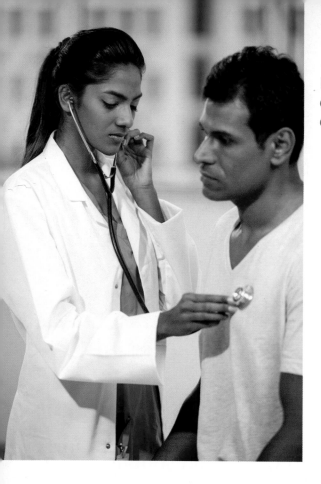

Staying Positive

Carrie's mom tried to reassure her. They didn't know yet if Aunt Sue had cancer. The doctor would do a number of tests to find out. And even if it did turn out to be cancer, that didn't mean Aunt Sue was going to die. Plenty of people get cancer, and there are lots of different treatments. If cancer is discovered early enough, many people make a full recovery. They would just have to wait and see what Aunt Sue's doctor had to say.

Aunt Sue got an appointment with her doctor the very next day. Carrie's mom was happy about that. She hoped it would turn out to be nothing, but she also knew that it is important to catch cancer early for the best chance at a successful treatment. She went to the appointment with Aunt Sue. After waiting a short time, they were shown into the doctor's private office.

Waiting to see a doctor can be stressful when a patient is worried about a serious illness like cancer.

A doctor might ask many questions to help figure out if a patient is at risk for cancer.

CHAPTER 2

Making a Diagnosis

The doctor asked Aunt Sue a number of questions. When had she discovered the lump? Had any of her close relatives ever had cancer? The doctor explained that some types of cancer seem to run in families, so if several relatives had been **diagnosed**, Sue might have a high cancer risk. The only way to find out if the lump was malignant (cancerous) or benign (not cancerous) was to do further tests.

 If you suspect that something is wrong, see your doctor as soon as possible.

Looking Inside the Body

After doing a physical exam, the doctor ordered a mammogram to find out more about the lump. A mammogram is a type of x-ray that can give an image of an area inside the breast. Another tool the doctor might use is an ultrasound. This is a test that uses sound waves to form an image of the suspicious area. X-rays, ultrasounds, and tests called magnetic resonance imaging (MRI) and computerized axial tomography (CAT) scans are also useful in diagnosing cancer.

Patients enter MRI machines through a tube-shaped opening.

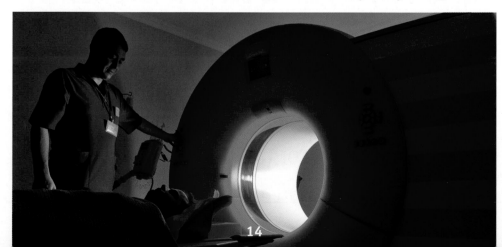

Radiologists are trained to notice signs of cancer and other problems when viewing images of a patient's body.

Aunt Sue had both a mammogram and an ultrasound of her breast. Once the tests were complete, the radiologist looked them over. Carrie's mom and Aunt Sue waited nervously for the results. When the radiologist returned, she had good news and bad news. The good news was that she didn't think the lump was cancer. The bad news was that she wasn't absolutely sure. To find out for certain, Sue would need a procedure called a biopsy.

Pathologists examine tissue samples to help diagnose many types of diseases.

Having a Biopsy

During a biopsy, an **anesthetic** is given to numb the patient's skin. Then a hollow needle is inserted into the area to be sampled. Sometimes, the doctor guides the needle to the correct spot by watching an ultrasound or x-rays of the procedure. Once the needle is in place, the doctor uses it to remove a small sample of tissue. By looking at the sample under a microscope, a pathologist can determine if it is cancerous.

Many Types of Tests

As we'll see later, there are many different kinds of cancer. There are also many ways to make a diagnosis. Some cancerous **tumors** release a substance that can be detected in a patient's blood. If these cancers are suspected, a blood test is performed. If the possible cancer is in the body cavity, in an organ such as the stomach or colon, a procedure known as an endoscopy can be used.

A blood test is sometimes the easiest way to determine if someone has cancer.

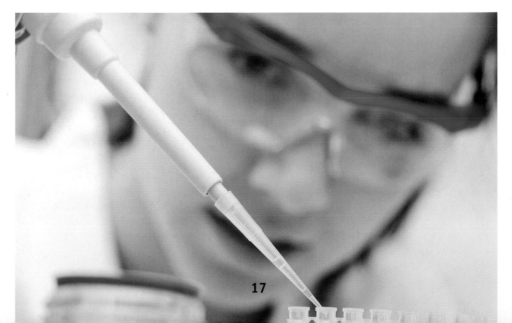

17

Surviving Cancer

A cancer diagnosis can be frightening. Many people think that having cancer means they are going to die. Fortunately, that's not true. There are many ways of treating cancer. Over the past few decades, many new treatments have been discovered. This means that more people than ever before can beat cancer. In 1962, only 4 percent of people diagnosed with leukemia (cancer of the blood) were alive five years after their diagnosis. Today, 94 percent of leukemia patients live for at least five years. Survival rates for many other cancers have increased as well.

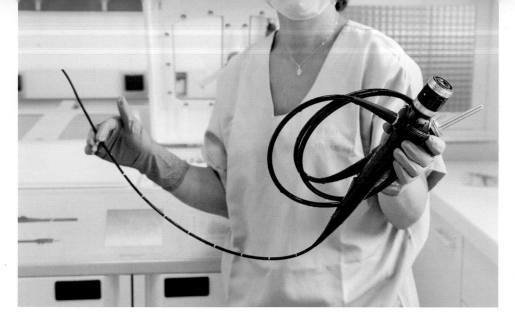

A surgeon holds up an endoscope.

Endoscopy

An endoscope is a thin, flexible tube with a small
camera and a bright light on the end. When it is
inserted into a body cavity, the endoscope sends
images to a screen to show the doctor what is going
on inside. If the doctor spots an unusual growth, he
can insert another tool through the endoscope and
collect cells to give to the pathologist. During the
procedure, a patient may be awake. Medicines numb
the affected area and help the patient stay relaxed.

Smoking: It's a Killer

Smoking cigarettes is extremely dangerous to your health. Smoking-related diseases include heart disease, lung disease, and several types of cancer. These illnesses kill an estimated 480,000 Americans each year. On average, smokers tend to die much earlier than nonsmokers—14.5 years earlier for women and 13.2 years earlier for men. However, smoking can affect nonsmokers. Breathing in the smoke of someone else's cigarette, called secondhand smoke, also increases a person's chance of developing health issues.

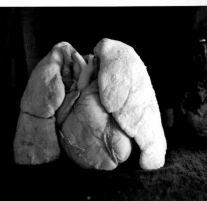

Despite these scary statistics, millions of people still smoke every day. Why? One reason is tobacco advertising,

which tries to make smoking seem fun and relaxing. In the United States, laws restrict the kinds of advertising tobacco companies can do. Some countries have banned tobacco advertising entirely.

Another reason some people keep smoking is nicotine, one of the substances in tobacco. Nicotine is highly addictive. This makes it very difficult to quit once a person starts smoking. People who suddenly quit smoking might feel sick until their body gets used to going without nicotine. The best way to avoid the effects of smoking? Don't start in the first place!

There are many different kinds of cells in the human body. Blood alone contains three basic types of cells: red blood cells, white blood cells, and platelets.

CHAPTER 3

The Causes of Cancer

Cancer is a disease that starts in the cells of the body. To understand cancer, we need to understand cells and what they do. Cells are the tiny building blocks of all living things. Your dog or cat, the plants outside, and your own body are all made up of cells. Similar cells group together to form different parts of your body: your skin, your blood, your bones, and so on. All the cells that make up your body work together to keep you alive.

Cells are made up of many individual parts.

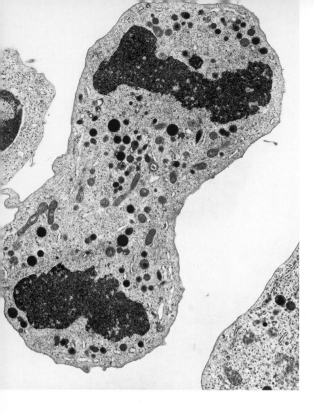

A bone marrow cell nears the end of the cell division process.

Cells Making New Cells

Eventually, every cell in your body wears out and dies. When a cell needs to be replaced, another cell splits into two, making an exact copy of itself. The process of replacing worn-out cells is called the cell cycle. In most cases, it works very well. But sometimes a cell doesn't know when to stop. It keeps making copies of itself, dividing over and over again in an uncontrolled way. This produces abnormal cells. They may clump together to form a tumor. Often these growths are harmless, but sometimes they are cancerous.

There are about 200 different cell types in the human body. Each does a specialized job. Cancer can occur in any of these cells, and this is why there are so many different types of cancer. The abnormal cells in a malignant tumor can invade neighboring areas. They may also break away and move through the bloodstream to other parts of the body. This is called **metastasis**. It is one of the main reasons that cancer is such a feared disease.

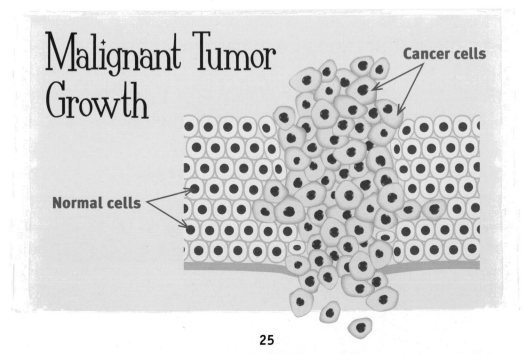

Malignant Tumor Growth

Cancer cells

Normal cells

Cells Gone Bad

What makes cells divide in an uncontrolled way in the first place? Why do most cells divide properly while others don't know when to stop? The simple answer is that some cells have been damaged in some way. As a result, that cell and the cells it produces no longer divide normally. This produces more abnormal, damaged cells. Different kinds of cancer have different causes. Cancer is not contagious. You cannot catch cancer from someone who has it. But exposure to harmful substances called carcinogens can injure cells. This causes them to make mistakes when they divide.

As cancer cells clump together, they can form tumors.

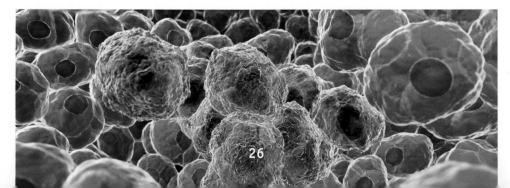

Children receive a mix of genes from both of their parents.

Who Gets Cancer?

There are a number of things that make it more likely that a person will get certain types of cancer. One of them is inheritance—that is, the **genes** people get from their parents. Genes are located on **chromosomes,** which are found inside every cell. They are the blueprints for things like your hair color, height, and other traits. If you inherit an abnormal gene from one or both of your parents, it can increase your chances of developing cancer under the right circumstances.

Because asbestos has been identified as a carcinogen, it is often removed from old buildings where it was used as insulation.

Smoke and Other Carcinogens

One of the best-known carcinogens is tobacco smoke. When a person inhales tobacco smoke, the lungs are exposed to thousands of chemical compounds, many of which have been shown to cause lung cancer. Other common substances in our environment have also been linked with cancer. These include asbestos (used in insulation), arsenic (in wood preservatives), formaldehyde (in building materials), BPA (in plastics, food containers, and drink cans), and many others.

A Weakened Immune System

Your body relies on its immune system to defend against infections, **viruses**, and other threats to your health. Some people have weak immune systems as a result of other illnesses or medical procedures. These people are less able to fight off viruses. Some types of cancer are caused by viruses. In people with weakened immune systems, a virus can more easily get out of control and cause changes to cells. This can eventually lead to cancer.

Epstein-Barr virus (below) has been linked to several types of cancer.

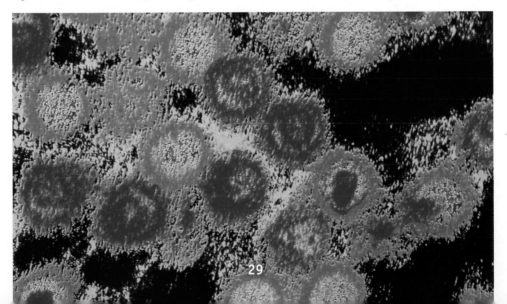

Age

Kids sometimes get cancer. Often, it begins to develop before the baby is born. However, cancer is much more common among adults. This is because the changes that turn a normal cell into a cancer cell take time to develop. The longer we live, the more time there is for mistakes to happen during cell division. Also, the longer we live, the more we are exposed to carcinogens. Smoking one cigarette will slightly increase your chance of developing lung cancer, but smoking cigarettes for 20 or 30 years will increase that chance dramatically.

Age increases a person's risk of developing cancer.

Wearing sunblock can help protect against skin cancer.

Lifestyle and Environment

Certain things that people do in their day-to-day lives can increase their risk of developing cancer. Spending too much time in the sun without sunblock can cause skin cancer. Eating too much red meat and processed foods, and not enough vegetables, can also increase cancer risk. So can being very overweight. Drinking too much alcohol may be linked to some cancers. Fortunately, the more you know about the causes of cancer, the easier it is to avoid them.

Cancer kills more people each year than AIDS, tuberculosis, and malaria combined.

Images and tissue samples of a cancerous tumor help doctors determine a patient's best course of treatment.

CHAPTER 4

Treating Cancer

When the results of Aunt Sue's biopsy came back, the news was good. The lump in her breast was benign. If it had been cancerous, however, the doctors could have done many things to treat it. When a person receives a cancer diagnosis, the first step is usually to see an oncologist. This doctor specializes in treating cancer. To decide on a treatment, the oncologist considers: the type of cancer, its location, how far it has progressed (called the stage), the patient's overall health, and his or her ability to tolerate side effects of treatment.

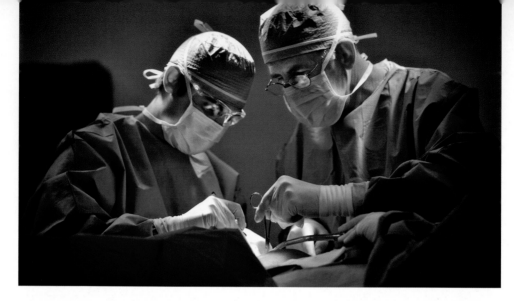

Surgery can be scary, but it is often the most effective way to deal with cancer.

Surgery

Removing cancerous tissue from the patient's body through surgery is the oldest form of cancer treatment. In addition to taking out the tumor itself, the surgeon usually removes some of the surrounding tissue to make sure all the cancer is gone. During surgery, the doctor may be able to see how far the cancer has advanced and whether it has spread to other areas of the body. Surgery is often just one step in cancer treatment.

Chemotherapy

Chemotherapy refers to the use of powerful drugs that target and kill cancer cells. It is often used in combination with surgery as a way of trying to ensure that all the cancer is gone from the body. Fast-growing cells like cancer cells are most affected by chemotherapy drugs. Unfortunately, other fast-growing cells, including those in the blood, intestines, mouth, and hair, are affected as well. Side effects such as hair loss, mouth sores, and blood disorders may result.

Chemotherapy can help shrink tumors, making them easier to remove with surgery.

Radiation

Radiation therapy use highs-energy x-rays to target cancer. The goal is to kill cancer cells without harming surrounding healthy tissue. In external beam therapy, computer programs are used to pinpoint the location of a tumor precisely. Then a machine directs a tightly focused beam of x-rays at the tumor. Radiation can also be delivered directly by surgically placing radioactive implants into or near the tumor.

Radiation must be carefully targeted at the affected area to avoid damaging other parts of the patient's body.

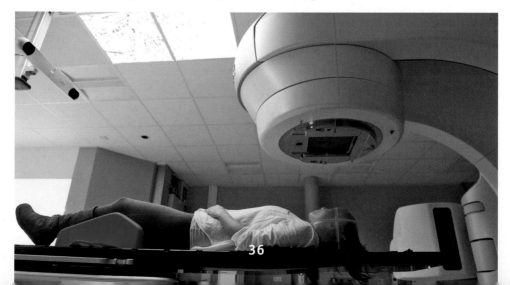

Cancer Vaccines

You have probably received vaccines to reduce the risk of getting diseases such as polio, measles, chicken pox, and even the flu. Did you know that you can also get a vaccine that will protect you from certain cancers? Vaccines work by training your immune system to recognize and destroy viruses and other harmful substances. Some cancers are caused by viruses. By vaccinating people against these viruses, doctors can prevent these cancers from developing.

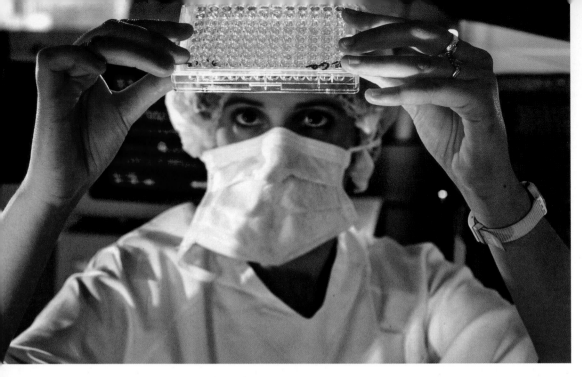

Scientists and doctors are constantly searching for new ways to use immunotherapy.

Immunotherapy

Immunotherapy uses the body's own defenses—the immune system—to fight disease. When confronted by a virus, infection, or some other invader, your immune system produces substances called antibodies to fight off the threat. Scientists have been able to make a variety of cancer antibodies in the laboratory.

These antibodies fight cancer in several ways. For example, they may attach to cancer cells, making it easier for the body's immune system to recognize and destroy the abnormal cells. Antibodies can also work by blocking the structures called growth factor receptors on the surface of cancer cells. With these receptors blocked, the cancer cells cannot continue to divide and grow.

An antibody (in blue) attached to a cancer cell (in orange) may make the cell more vulnerable to the body's natural defenses.

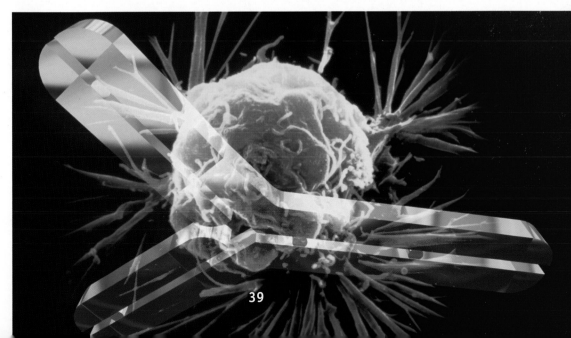

Hearing that treatment is
working is the best news a
cancer patient can receive.

CHAPTER 5

Life After Cancer

Cancer is a serious disease, but it doesn't have to be fatal. Many factors influence a cancer patient's chances of survival. These include the type of cancer, where it is located in the body, and how advanced the cancer is when it is discovered. Another important factor is whether the cancer has spread to other parts of the body. A person's age, general health, and how well he or she responds to treatment also affect chances of survival.

Breast cancer is about 100 times more common in women than in men.

Remission

If, after cancer treatment, the signs of a person's cancer disappear or are reduced, the person is said to be in remission. Even after treatment, some cancer cells may remain hidden in the body. They can cause the cancer to come back one day. Most cancer patients see their doctors regularly after their cancer treatments have finished. The doctor monitors their progress and does tests to check for signs that the cancer may be returning.

Regular visits to a doctor are important for recovering cancer patients.

Each birthday following remission places a patient one step closer to being declared cancer-free.

For most cancer patients, the first five years after treatment are very important. If the cancer returns, it is most likely to happen during these first few years. Every year that a patient remains cancer free is a milestone. If there is still no sign of cancer after five years, some doctors will say that the person is cancer-free. As new treatments are developed, the hope is that more and more people will survive cancer in years to come. ★

True Statistics

Number of cells in the body of an adult human being: About 37 trillion

Number of cells that die and are replaced each minute in an adult human being: 96 million

Number of chemicals in cigarette smoke shown to cause cancer: More than 70

Percent of cancer deaths caused by tobacco use: 22

Percent of deaths in the world caused by cancer: About 12.5; that's 1 in 8 people

Percent of cancers diagnosed in people 55 years old or older: 77

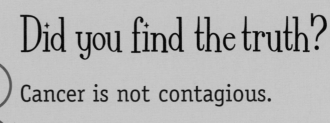

Did you find the truth?

(T) Cancer is not contagious.

(F) Cancer is always fatal.

Resources

Books

Casil, Amy Sterling. *Pancreatic Cancer: Current and Emerging Trends in Detection and Treatment*. New York: Rosen, 2009.

Glader, Sue. *Nowhere Hair*. Mill Valley, CA: Thousand Words Press, 2010.

Orr, Tamra. *Liver Cancer: Current and Emerging Trends in Detection and Treatment*. New York: Rosen, 2009.

Simons, Rae. *Cancer & Kids*. Vestal, NY: AlphaHouse, 2009.

Visit this Scholastic Web site for more information on cancer:

★ www.factsfornow.scholastic.com
Enter the keyword **Cancer**

Important Words

anesthetic (an-us-THET-ik) — a drug given to people to prevent or lessen pain

chromosomes (KROH-muh-sohmz) — the structures inside a cell that carry the genes that give living things their individual characteristics

diagnosed (dye-uhg-NOSD) — determined what disease a patient has or what the cause of a problem is

genes (JEENZ) — the parts that make up chromosomes and are passed from parents to children, influencing how they look and grow

metastasis (muh-TAS-tuh-sus) — the spread of something that produces disease (as cancer cells) from its original location to another part of the body

radiation (ray-dee-AY-shuhn) — atomic particles that are sent out from a radioactive substance and can be used to fight cancer

tumors (TOO-murz) — abnormal lumps or masses of cells in the body

viruses (VYE-ruhs-iz) — very tiny organisms that can reproduce and grow only when inside living cells; viruses cause diseases such as polio, measles, the common cold, and AIDS

Index

Page numbers in **bold** indicate illustrations.

About the Author

Ann O. Squire is a psychologist and an animal behaviorist. Before becoming a writer, she studied the behavior of rats, tropical fish in the Caribbean, and electric fish from central Africa. Her favorite part of being a writer is the chance to learn as much as she can about all sorts of topics. In addition to *Cancer* and books on other health topics, Dr. Squire has written about many different animals, from lemmings to leopards and cicadas to cheetahs. She lives in Long Island City, New York.